What Our Readers Have Said...

"Although I consider myself a seasoned sales professional, it is helpful to have past learning's refreshed. The books were also beneficial because of the information concerning 'trends' in the sales relationship. The sales process should be viewed as dynamic since business relationships change regularly."

•

"For the particular business I am in and the type of sales calls I have, I find that the books in the Pinpoint Sales Training Series are very often applicable to how I conduct business. I would recommend them to other sales people, just not ones that are in my industry."

•

"These books provide very good concepts. It fits in well with the Bell Leadership training program that I attended in November."

•

"I use this material in these books and apply it to my customers and other employees I work with."

•

"I would like to know other topics. Is there anything on Production Management or Consultative Selling or Time Management?"

•

"These books are great tools that should be used as guidelines for our everyday

supervisory practices. You need to take the time to do a short self-evaluation when reading them."

•

"The Pinpoint Training Series delivers information that could be used in a lot different areas."

•

"I like this because I can take them with me to read at a convenient time. I feel the little time I have to spend in the office is best use on activities that directly relate to revenue opportunities. I like the short amount of time it takes to keep up with these."

•

"I prefer the self-study approach; it fits in with my schedule."

•

"My thought is that the real value of these books comes into effect when doing the action plans."

•

"Short and sweet. These books are easy to comprehend."

•

"I have enjoyed reading these books. They are relevant to today's work environment and the ongoing change in the way we manage our workforce."

•

"I do feel that these books have been very helpful to me at my job."

•

"I think a lot of the recommendations in these books are very useful, and can be applicable to everyday situations. If nothing else, it's a good reference guide to fall back upon if a situation arises in the future."

•

"These books are relevant to today's work environment and the ongoing change in the way we manage our workforce."

•

Productive Sales Planning

Pinpoint Sales Skill Development Training Series

TIMOTHY F. BEDNARZ

MAJORIUM
BUSINESS PRESS

Pinpoint Sales Skill Development Training Series
"Productive Sales Planning"
Timothy F. Bednarz

Graphic design: Monika Pawlak

Majorium Business Press
2025 Main Street
Stevens Point, WI 54481
715.342.1018 • 800.654.4935

ISBN 978-1-882181-72-8

Printed in the United States of America

Introduction

The Pinpoint Sales Skill Development Training Series is designed for targeted training and education regarding increased improvement in a specific skill or competency.

Each book within this series is designed to be easy to use, understand and apply to your job. It can be used as a basis for training individuals, as a discussion guide or as a personal training tool.

Each chapter within this book discusses a specific concept. When you have completed all eight chapters you should have a 360° perspective of the topic.

Additionally, each chapter is divided into specific sections:

- The first section provides you with an overview of the topic
- The Implications section discusses why the concept is important, and why it is important to learn and apply.
- The Strategies, Tips & Techniques to Apply section teaches how to use and apply the particular concept to your work.
- The Points to Ponder section gives you something to think about or to be discussed with a group setting. These are questions not meant to be immediately answered, but to be pondered over time.
- The Training Activity section provides you with the tools to transfer what you have learned to your job. It is designed to help create an action plan to effectively apply the concept.

Each of the topics in this series is time-tested and proven in the marketplace. They have been used by thousands of employees as training tools. Many of the users have commented that what made these books valuable, was the ability to refer to them when a problem surfaced. They indicated that they remembered reading about the exact problem. They referred back to these books and found an appropriate solution.

You will find them equally valuable as a resource in your professional development library.

Table of Contents

LEARNING OBJECTIVES:

- To understand the need for planning.
- To determine the effective use of their personal resources.
- To analyze their past sales performance.
- To establish personal goals and objectives.
- To develop an effective sales plan.
- To implement their sales plans and put them into action.

1

What a Territory Analysis Should Tell You

In a territory analysis, salespeople and managers start to examine the current year's sales performance and begin looking forward to next year. While many salespeople feel this is a wasted effort on their part, it does have a true and identifiable value to them.

A number of problems and issues can be revealed in a comprehensive territory analysis that are symptomatic of the need for additional managerial training, direction and/or coaching. Sales managers need to address these issues during their reviews with individual salespeople.

IMPLICATIONS – WHAT THIS MEANS TO YOU

Many salespeople suffer through the annual planning cycle and consider the exercise unproductive. However, with salesmen and women so intensely focused on their customers and new business development, little time is left to plan and reflect on overall progress.

Beyond a cursory examination of key sales indicators, a regular review affords the salesperson the opportunity to stand back and review a number of other factors significantly affecting their performance.

STRATEGIES, TIPS & TECHNIQUES TO APPLY

Indicative of ineffective selling behaviors, any of the following five critical problems can surface in a territory analysis:

Poor Customer Coverage

A sales representative with a customer coverage problem may find it is due to poor time management and business development skills. Poor customer coverage is identified by two primary factors:

- An inability to maintain established call frequencies
- An undesirable number of complaints and requests for sales service

The cause of an inordinate number of requests for sales service must be ascertained in order to establish whether the salesperson is the problem or if there are post-sales and customer service issues. If an internal service problem exists, it should be present over more than one territory; if not, there may be a problem with the salesperson's ability to develop business relationships and adequately educate and train customers in the proper use and application of their product.

Inadequate New Customer Development

New sales development is a critical sales skill. Without sufficient sales prospects in the pipeline, salespeople will be unable to meet the goals set in their sales plans. A problem in this area indicates that an individual salesperson requires training and coaching to develop their prospecting and cold calling skills.

Unbalanced Selling of Several Product Lines

Analysis may reveal an unbalanced selling of several products rather than a full coverage of the entire product line. The mix of companies and industries located within a specific sales territory may dictate a lack of sales balance. Analysis may also indicate several additional sales-related problems, including:

- The inability to present and push new products

- High-spotting
- A neglect of individual products

Unbalanced selling habits may indicate a lack of motivation or self-confidence on the part of the salesperson. Salespeople can have such a high degree of success selling a specific product or line that rather than venture into new and unknown lines, they stress only the areas in which they are most comfortable. Intensive training in the development of product knowledge will be required to encourage these individuals to sell across the entire product line.

Wide Differences in Competitive Positions

Sales managers often identify wide differences in competitive positions when they compare their analysis of several sales territories. This problem is indicative of the salesperson skimming their territory or highlighting major accounts while failing to develop the overall potential of the territory. In some instances the territory may simply be too lucrative for an individual salesperson to cover.

This problem can be complicated by an unbalanced sales approach requiring that the salesperson's territory be divided, additional salespeople added or portions of territory added to less lucrative areas.

Poor Balancing of Sales Potential

Poor balancing of the available sales potential within a territory is directly related to the personal effectiveness of the salesperson. Ineffectiveness points to poor sales and time management skills and can also indicate an overall lack of motivation.

After carefully evaluating the causes of poor performance, the sales manager must take corrective steps—often including intensive training and coaching—to bring the salesperson up to a level of acceptable performance.

POINTS TO PONDER – SOMETHING TO THINK ABOUT

1. Are there any problems with your performance, specifically identified by these factors?
2. Can you think of ways to modify your sales style after reviewing these five factors?

TRAINING ACTIVITY – APPLICATION & ACTION PLAN

1. Conduct a preliminary territory review and compare it with your sales goals for this year.
2. Determine how your customer list has changed.
3. Review your product mix.
4. After a preliminary review, determine if there are any indicators in the following areas:
    - Poor Customer Coverage
    - Inadequate New Customer Development
    - Unbalanced Selling of Several Product Lines
    - Wide Differences in Competitive Positions
    - Poor Balancing of Sales Potential

2

The Territory Analysis

A territory analysis can be compared to a giant, filtered funnel: the sales representative develops an overall database of information, "pours" it into the funnel and analyzes it, and usable information comes out of the narrow end.

Today, managers are awash in information, but starving for usable information. Territory analysis gives salespeople and managers the tools to provide the specific information needed to effectively manage their sales assets.

IMPLICATIONS – WHAT THIS MEANS TO YOU

Providing innumerable benefits, an effective territory analysis examines the entire scope of existing business while conducting a regular review of the business opportunities that exist and have been created since the last sales evaluation.

Many salespeople tend to skim their territories. A territory analysis allows sales managers to discuss the potential that exists in their people's territory while identifying future opportunities that will help meet the goals of the company. This ensures that the activities of individual sales representatives are in line with the overall goals of the company.

A territory analysis identifies and targets customer segments by product and application. Managers long assuming their company's success flowed from their product portfolio are now realizing the true source of value lies within their *customer* portfolios.

One of a company's most valuable and typically underutilized assets is the customer portfolio. The development, analysis and management of customer portfolios allows a company of any size to harness a powerful source of growth and profitability. An effective territory analysis provides for the management of this asset.

When salespeople conduct an effective territory analysis, they are able to identify not only the most profitable customers to invest their time, but also an accurate sales forecast based upon the probability of obtaining a prospect's business. Their territory forecast determines the overall profitability of the territory.

Additionally, a territory analysis benchmarks the competitive activities occurring within the territory. This identifies the individual segments they serve and determines the best practices to use to acquire and keep customers. Salespeople can systematically modify their strategies to adopt the best practices of their competition.

When completed, a territory analysis provides the salesperson and their manager with a strategic tool to develop sales strategies and plans and determine how best to counter competitive activities.

STRATEGIES, TIPS & TECHNIQUES TO APPLY

There are six steps to follow in conducting an effective territory analysis. The process begins with the sales representative assembling and collecting all available information and data about their territory, including sales records, call reports, competitive information and a host of other related materials.

Once the information is collected, the next step is to analyze and distill it into meaningful output to use in making key decisions for effective sales planning.

The output of a territory analysis allows salespeople to determine the potential business within their territory. This potential business is then prioritized so that they can target and focus upon the most profitable accounts and customer segments.

The purpose of a territory analysis is to enable salespeople to concentrate their efforts on the most profitable businesses in their territory, thus allowing them to invest their time and resources where it will have the greatest impact on sales and commissions.

The core of any analysis lies in developing data on each individual account. This individual breakdown facilitates the compiling of accurate information. As salespeople go through this planning process, this information can be used to develop key numbers. It will then be used for the development of account plans for key customers and prospects.

Additional analysis should be conducted to determine the sales activity within the territory for the past year. This is comparable to a financial balance sheet for the sales territory. Weighing the positive against negative factors over the past year, it becomes an indicator of the financial health of the territory and the salesperson's performance.

The first factor—New Business Activity—identifies what has occurred over the past year. New business development is essential for the viability and growth of every business.

The second factor is Lost Business Activity. The fact that every business loses accounts for a variety of reasons over the course of a year calls increased attention to the issue of customer retention. A Harvard Business School study showed that a 2% annual retention of existing customers contributes an additional 10% net profit for the business. Therefore it is important to analyze exactly where and why business has been lost.

The final factor, Key Account Activity, is a synopsis of key account activity during the past year.

Where the initial analysis is a statement of past performance, the territory analysis produces a forecast of future performance for the upcoming year, including:

- New business
- Changes in key account activity
- Changes in gross margins

- Lost business
- Existing customers' buying habits
- Ways products are utilized
- Need for other products and services

POINTS TO PONDER — SOMETHING TO THINK ABOUT

1. Do you view territory analysis as a planning resource? Why? How have you approached it in the past?
2. List areas in the various phases of sales planning you have found helpful in your past sales efforts.

TRAINING ACTIVITY — APPLICATION & ACTION PLAN

1. List the following factors on a sheet of paper:
    - New Business Activity
    - Lost Business Activity
    - Key Account Activity
2. List all changes you have noticed over the past year in each of these areas.

3

Identification of Changes and Opportunities in Your Sales Territory

A sales analysis is the systematic process of collecting, organizing, evaluating and interpreting actual sales data for the purpose of projecting performance for the period ahead. Its purpose is to uncover significant trends and relationships in order to take action to improve future performance.

Effective sales analysis is explanatory and proscriptive by nature. It should reflect good judgment in the selection of factors to be considered as well as clear cause-and-effect thinking in findings and conclusions. Finally, it provides sound information and recommendations for action to improve sales and profit performance. It should be noted that a sales plan is no better than the sales forecasts upon which the plans are based.

IMPLICATIONS – WHAT THIS MEANS TO YOU

Many salespeople show disdain for the principles of effective sales planning. They'll plan a party or a vacation, but they hate to plan the one element that can dramatically impact their income potential.

When the economy is sputtering and rife with uncertainty, proactive sales planning and analysis becomes not only important but also indispensable to the sustained success of the individual salesperson.

Times of uncertainty are filled with opportunity. The greatest fortunes have been made as societies have made major shifts, with the Industrial Age producing names such as Rockefeller, Carnegie and Krupp, and the Technological Age spawning individuals such as Bill Gates and Steve Jobs.

Salespeople who know that many unique and lucrative opportunities can only be uncovered by utilizing professional skills, expertise and discipline make a serious investment in sales analysis and planning.

STRATEGIES, TIPS & TECHNIQUES TO APPLY

As salespeople invest the time in sales analysis and planning, the following key changes and opportunities should be identified and summarized.

New Business

Forecasted new business for the upcoming year should be defined by the following criteria:

- The source of new business
- The product mix
- The gross margins contributed by the new business

Changes in Key Account Activity

Forecasted changes in key account activities for the upcoming year are identified using the following criteria:

- Key account
- Sales
- Change in sales from previous year
- Profit margin contribution

Changes in Gross Margins

Answering the question, "What are the forecasted changes in gross margin contributions for the upcoming year?" determines whether or not there is a shift toward increasing productivity within the territory. Salespeople should ideally be looking for ways to sell or up-sell accounts to increase the overall profit contribution of the products sold.

Lost Business

The anticipated business to be lost for a variety of reasons, from plant closings to competitive activity, should be determined using the following criteria:

- Customer
- Type
- Cause
- Competitive activity

Existing Customers' Buying Habits

An analysis should be developed detailing the buying habits of existing customers, notably the major accounts within the territory. This is performed to identify trends and shifts in buying habits within the territory.

Ways Customers Use Products

Customers, their needs and the way they use products are constantly changing. This analysis views the trends and shifts in the application of the products and services sold.

Need for Other Products and Services

This analysis identifies products and services the company does not directly supply but are nevertheless requested or needed by customers and prospects. This is information to be used by the marketing and product development departments for future product development ideas.

Results

The sales analysis should target specific results that make this information meaningful in the planning and development of the territory. The targeted results should include:

Organization of Sales into Significant Segments – Data should be analyzed and organized into significant and meaningful segments. These can be classified into customer or product groups, depending upon the nature of the territory.

Cross-Classification or Correlation – The cross-classification or correlation of analyzed data is useful for bringing out meaningful relationships. As data never exists in a void, critical elements must be cross-linked to develop trends and extrapolate the meaning of what the information is actually conveying. The more individual factors included into an analysis, the more meaningful it will be.

Market Share – Market share can be determined by reviewing the sales potential of a territory and extrapolating competitive accounts and their sales potential.

Adverse Trends – A summary of the sales analysis should detect any adverse trends within the territory. This is performed by correlating lost business, key account activities and the market share data of the territory while extrapolating current trends. Adverse trends are earmarked for action during the strategy development phase.

POINTS TO PONDER — SOMETHING TO THINK ABOUT

1. How extensively have you analyzed your sales activities and performance in the past?
2. Does economic uncertainty prompt and motivate you to plan your upcoming year's activities more carefully?

TRAINING ACTIVITY — APPLICATION & ACTION PLAN

1. Objectively examine the factors affecting your sales territory. On a sheet a paper create two columns labeled "Positive Trends" and "Negative Trends." Along the left side of the page list the following:
    - Economic
    - Industry
    - Company
    - Customer
    - Product
2. Describe next to each item the adverse and/or positive trends affecting your sales territory.
3. Formulate strategies for maximizing or countering each of these trends.

4

The Development of Specific Goals and Objectives Details the Sales Plan

The basis of any sales plan must be consistent with the overall sales and marketing goals of the company. One obvious goal is for salespeople to reach the sales quota set by management.

The salesperson must use the information developed during the assessment stage of his or her territory to create specific sales goals for the year. They then set objectives, or the specific steps they will take to achieve those goals.

IMPLICATIONS — WHAT THIS MEANS TO YOU

Successful sales planning details the specific actions a salesperson needs to take during the year to achieve his or her goals and objectives. Often sales plans only specify the volume a salesperson intends to achieve without the specific actions and activities that are required to be successful. Additionally, many plans fall short because the projected sales volumes are either baseless or are developed simply by adding a percentage to the past year's sales volume.

Effective sales planning develops a detailed roadmap for salespeople to follow. Successfully implemented, salespeople should easily achieve their goals and objectives, as rather than a large and possibly unachievable annual target, goals have been broken down into smaller and more readily achieved steps. This keeps individual representatives continually focused on desired results; otherwise many only begin to focus on their goals at the end of the year. The accomplishment of sales goals should be a daily focus, only achieved with effective planning techniques.

Success builds upon success: when salespeople achieve daily, weekly and monthly goals, confidence and motivation builds. Salespeople need to avoid planning their activities too tightly. A 20% cushion should be allowed for unplanned and uncontrollable events and opportunities.

STRATEGIES, TIPS & TECHNIQUES TO APPLY

The salesperson must create a specific strategy to reach their sales goals and objectives. An effective sales strategy should incorporate the following elements:

Overall sales territory strategy – The total strategy the salesperson intends to use within his or her sales territory.

Specific product strategy – Determines the product mix of the territory by focusing on the sale of the most profitable products to the salesperson's customers and their applications. This strategy will vary from territory to territory.

Specific competitive strategy – Determines specific sales strategies to be activated and employed in order to counter the competition. This strategy maximizes the company's strengths in the territory while minimizing the competition.

Specific customer strategy – Includes the sales plan for each targeted and potential customer. It is essential that a particular sales plan be developed for each targeted account. These plans should include:

- A specific strategy for the account
- Account goals and objectives
- Product goals and objectives
- A sales plan and objectives for the account
- A call plan and objectives for the account

- Objectives of each call
- A timeline for the sale

Implementation

The sales plan must detail how each goal, objective and strategy will be implemented. Each step should be detailed so the salesperson has a blueprint to follow to achieve their goals and objectives.

Evaluation

A sales plan should have various benchmarks and milestones. This is needed for the salesperson to monitor their actual performance against their projected goals and objectives. Benchmarks and milestones should be established with the sales manager early and frequently enough to allow for corrective action if problems occur or performance lags.

Adaptation

The final step is to adapt the sales plan to actual market conditions and results. No plan is perfect, and every plan will need to be changed, modified or altered along the way.

Additionally, as it is a constantly evolving process, a plan is never fully realized. The salesperson needs to work the plan, and reassess and reestablish goals and objectives on a regular and frequent basis.

Time Frame

The most important aspect of the sales strategy is the initial plan. This is when each step is detailed completely. Once completed, the sales plan should be revisited quarterly, whereupon all elements should be analyzed for any changes including new customers, competitors or alterations in the sales environment.

A more comprehensive review should be conducted annually, with the entire process repeated every two to three years.

POINTS TO PONDER – SOMETHING TO THINK ABOUT

1. Have your past sales plans set specific and achievable goals and objectives?
2. How much time and effort do you normally invest in your sales plans?

TRAINING ACTIVITY – APPLICATION & ACTION PLAN

1. Identify one major sales account for the upcoming sales year.
2. Develop the following for this account:
   - A specific strategy for the account
   - Account goals and objectives
   - Product goals and objectives
   - A sales plan and objectives for the account
   - A call plan and objectives for the account
   - Objectives of each call
   - A timeline for the sale

5

Effective Sales Strategies Build Competitive Immunity

When salespeople are successful in building long-term relationships, they create competitive immunity for themselves. This occurs because they have taken the time to analyze and diagnose the customer's business and educate them as to the effective, value-added solutions available to their business.

Competitive immunity occurs when the salesperson and their company are viewed as being indispensable to the customer. The customer understands that the value being delivered will be difficult, if not impossible, to duplicate, and that a decision to change could materially harm their business. At this point the salesperson and his or her company are *in* business with the customer, not just *doing* business with them.

IMPLICATIONS — WHAT THIS MEANS TO YOU

How many salespeople really develop a complete understanding of their individual customers? Many salespeople are too busy getting to the next sale to fully understand what the customer really wants from them.

The days of hit-and-run selling are over. Customers have become more sophisticated—and are demanding the same from their vendors. Salespeople who can completely understand the needs of the customer and address those needs with their product or service are the ones who get the sale.

This is important to the salesperson because competitive immunity does not come about without a strategic commitment.

STRATEGIES, TIPS & TECHNIQUES TO APPLY

Salespeople must take the time to develop precise strategies to make competitive immunity a reality. Effective sales strategies are the result of a comprehensive understanding of the customer's specific needs and how they can best be met in a competitive sales environment. Some of the critical issues that need to be addressed include:

What Are the Customer's Needs?

Some customers know exactly what they want and need; others do not. It is up to the salesperson to assess the customer's real needs through persistent questioning and careful analysis of their responses.

What Are the Problems?

The problems the customer is facing are often the first indicators of their needs. Problems often compel the customer to make a change in their method of business. When problems are identified, the salesperson can begin to fashion solutions.

What Are the Opportunities?

Opportunities are assessed by visiting and talking to the customer, users and anyone involved with the use of their product. These actions will often paint a complete picture of what is happening as well as openings that can be taken advantage of. Salespeople who visit, talk, look and listen will be surprised by the opportunities that become available.

Are There Any Limitations?

Limitations can take many forms during any given sale. Salespeople must work within budgets, time frames, facilities and operational limitations. All sales have some from of constraints affecting how a product can solve the customer's problem. It is up to the salesperson to determine what those limitations are and how to work around and overcome them.

Determining the Real Buyer of the Product/Service

Salespeople typically deal with middle-level managers or purchasing agents throughout the bulk of the selling process. These people are often only screening information for the actual buyer or decision maker. Whenever possible it is important to get beyond the screener to talk with the actual decision maker. This will make the process go smoother and probably shorten the sales cycle.

Additionally, people other than the actual buyer generally use the product, and it is important to gather their feedback. These individuals usually have immediate access and input to the sales process without the salesperson knowing about it. Dealing with these individuals minimizes the chances of being blindsided by a group's agenda or other unforeseen factors. Some questions to address when dealing with these constituencies include:

> *What Are They Seeking?* – Salespeople generally don't have direct contact with these hidden groups and, as such, won't be able to determine their needs. The screener often does not know what is specifically involved in the product's application and cannot provide accurate information. Thus salespeople need to see the actual users and determine their specific needs and agendas.
>
> *What Are They Expecting from the Product?* – The meeting of expectations is critical to the long-term success of a relationship with that customer. The screener may have no knowledge of the expectations of the decision maker or final customer. Gatekeepers might be able to furnish the screening specifications. It is up to the salesperson to determine the actual expectations of these subgroups that control the buying process.
>
> *What Are the Solutions?* – Once the salesperson has discovered actual needs and expectations, they are able to craft a solution tailored to meet these particular requirements. The alternative is to meet general specifications and quote a price that will be compared in a light that is potentially unfavorable to the salesperson.

How Does the Solution Meet Their Expectations? – It is critical that solutions be tailored to specifically meet the expectations of the actual constituencies responsible for the buying decision. The more adept that salespeople are in crafting their solution to meet end-users' expectations, the more it places them in a favorable light and negates the pure price bidding process originally proposed by the customer.

POINTS TO PONDER – SOMETHING TO THINK ABOUT

1. How specific have your sales strategies been in meeting the needs of your customers and creating competitive immunity?
2. Have you created competitive immunity with any of your customers?

TRAINING ACTIVITY – APPLICATION & ACTION PLAN

Identify a major customer and prospect. Use the following criteria to establish a sales strategy for this account.

- What are the needs of the customer?
- What are the problems?
- What are the opportunities?
- Are there any limitations?
    - Determine the real buyer and customer for your product.
    - What is the customer specifically seeking from you?
    - What is the customer expecting to obtain from your product?
    - What are your solutions?
    - How does your solution meet their expectations?

6

Developing the Individual Sales Plans

Through active participation in the development of sales plans, salespeople gain knowledge, insight and understanding. In each sales plan, goals and plans of individual salespeople are brought into harmony with the overall objectives of the company. Most importantly, plans are based on hard data and facts, not supposition.

IMPLICATIONS – WHAT THIS MEANS TO YOU

The most difficult aspect of developing any plan is the collection and analysis of facts. But unless properly done, the plan will be unrealistic and unattainable.

The sales plan brings all of the elements of the territorial, sales and competitive analysis into focus. Within these sections, data on the salesperson's past performance is collected and analyzed. The individual selling strengths and weaknesses can be evaluated based upon this analysis and the status of current sales projects established.

Such an analysis allows the sales representative and manager to identify the most promising opportunities and isolate the most serious problems requiring immediate attention. It shows the salesperson how to use their strengths and available resources to their competitive advantage.

Once completed, the analysis and forecasts allow the sales representative to set challenging, realistic and achievable goals for the upcoming year. It details the specific tasks necessary to accomplish these goals, sets timelines and targets responsibilities.

Development of an adequate sales plan requires precise knowledge on the part of the salesperson concerning their company, products, competition and customers. It is this specific knowledge that seasons the plan and makes it achievable.

STRATEGIES, TIPS & TECHNIQUES TO APPLY

The key elements to be included in the sales plan include:

Identification and Quantification of the Market Served

The sales plan should include the entire scope of the market served. The following elements should be identified and quantified:

- Sales
- Monthly bookings
- Targeted markets
- Market share
- Sales by customer segment
- Sales by product
- Key account activity

Objectives with Assumptions

Sales goals and objectives should be detailed for the upcoming year. Supporting data for the goals and objectives should include:

- Strategic goals and objectives for the year
- Tactical goals and objectives by month
- Profit objectives

- Key assumptions
- Benchmarks

Strategies to Follow

Strategies that are to be followed by the salesperson for the year should be detailed, including:

- Overall sales strategies
- Strategies for new business development
- Strategies for key account activity
- Time management strategies

Product Emphasis

The product emphasis within the territory should be specified, including:

- Key product segments
- Major product emphasis
- Product mix
- New product emphasis
- Product profitability forecast

Targeted Accounts

The salesperson should detail the targeted accounts for the year, including:

- Name of account
- Targeted products
- Targeted profitability
- Key account activity

Bookings and Sales Budget

Sales plans should include a comprehensive annual sales budget broken down by month, including bookings and sales by:

- Key accounts
- Customer segments
- Products
- Profitability

Market Outlook Report

Conveying information and potential trends concerning customers, competitors and other market influences, the market outlook report should include:

- Customers' and prospects' expansion plans, personnel changes, new products, etc.
- Information about competitor's price changes, new products, personnel changes
- Information about other market influences such as legislation, regulation and the effects of the economy or weather on the market

Sales Expense Budget

The sales plan should include an expense budget for the year broken down by each month, including:

- Commissions
- Sales expenses
- Travel
- Time

Accountability

The sales plan should contain factors to measure the salesperson's performance and hold them accountable for their actions against their plan. This should include the individual performance factors being measured against the plan and the reasons why.

This is to be specified with month-to-month quotas that can be compared with actual sales performance to-date. In addition to monthly quotas, a detailed list of scheduled calls and key account activity together with the expected results should be available. New business to be targeted and the anticipated timeline to close this business should also be detailed.

Finally, a travel plan should be developed that outlines the time allocated by account, including anticipated travel time for the year.

POINTS TO PONDER — SOMETHING TO THINK ABOUT

1. Cite examples where you have used either invalid historical data or suppositions in the development of your sales plans.
2. Explain what the results were when you attempted to short-circuit the planning process.

TRAINING ACTIVITY — APPLICATION & ACTION PLAN

Begin the process of developing your sales plans by performing the following activities:

1. List the resources you will require to successfully develop and complete your sales plan.
2. Prioritize the resources you will require and can realistically expect to receive from your company.

7

Developing Account Plans

Many salespeople have a sales strategy because they are required to, but few will have an account plan and sales strategy developed for each major prospect.

Knowing that it's often what the competition fails to do that makes the difference, salespeople with the initiative to consistently develop and follow account plans create a distinct competitive advantage for themselves.

IMPLICATIONS – WHAT THIS MEANS TO YOU

The individual account plan addresses the same elements of customer, product and competitive knowledge that are taken into consideration when creating an overall sales strategy. In crafting unique sales solutions that maximize company and product strengths while minimizing their weaknesses, the plan both specifically details how the individual needs of the customer will be met and strategically positions the salesperson against the competition.

Most salespeople prioritize their prospects and customers into "A," "B" or "C" accounts, but few develop account plans for their major accounts.

The data a salesperson collects needs to be written down and collated. Memorizing information does not allow one to view it objectively and arrive at conclusions and strategies for effectively selling and maintaining an account. Each piece of information collected is a "piece of the puzzle," and it is up to salespeople to assemble that puzzle into a cohesive account plan.

STRATEGIES, TIPS & TECHNIQUES TO APPLY

Every sale requires extensive preparation. Salespeople need to perform significant legwork to collect and compile the information required to develop effective account plans. In order to create a competitive advantage, salespeople should:

Determine Wants, Needs, Desires

Good salespeople take the time to find out what their prospects are looking for and why by asking thoughtful questions, *listening* carefully, and maintaining a focus on what the customer is saying and how they say it.

Salespeople will find that a careful needs analysis may cause them to lose prospects that don't really need their product but help them hold on to those who do. Salespeople need to show prospects they care about their particular wants and needs. In this manner, trust is established and the salesperson secures a foundation upon which to build a lasting business relationship.

Determine Prospect's Financial Status

While finances may be a sensitive issue, salespeople need to have some idea of a prospect's capacity to purchase. They need to ask for a ballpark range that will help them tailor solutions to the prospect's budgetary constraints. Salespeople might want to determine the prospect's budget for next year in order to ascertain whether they will have more buying power in the future.

Identify All Decision Makers

If salespeople are going to prepare a compelling presentation that will yield a sale, they must make sure all the right people hear it. Salespeople need to ask for the names and titles of everyone involved in purchasing decisions.

Establish a Buying Time Frame

Salespeople need to determine when the prospect might be ready to make a buying decision. Salespeople should develop a schedule of phone calls, appointments and presentation dates so that both parties can prepare for each contact. In so doing salespeople can anticipate approximately when they might expect a decision.

Uncover the Competition

Salespeople should query prospects as to additional competitive products they might be considering. A needs analysis determines the requirements competitive offerings meet versus the salesperson's own offering.

Eliminate Objections

A properly qualified prospect is the best defense against objections later in the sales process. If there is a need and the prospect can afford the product or service, there is no reason why a competent salesperson cannot make the sale.

Before salespeople invest time and effort in their prospects, they make certain to properly qualify them in order to provide the most optimal chances of a return.

Many salespeople attribute objections and rejection to ineffective presentations or the inability to close, but often the reason is that they simply failed to properly qualify the prospect in the first place.

Gather Information for Follow-Up

Salespeople need to gather as much information as possible about their prospect's business beforehand so they can use the information collected to help them after the actual sale.

Salespeople should continually ask questions of the prospect's business: how they operate, their goals, recurring problems, expectations. Establishing themselves as experts on their customers' industries and businesses adds value to the overall sale.

Account plans help salespeople compile the information collected, analyze it and develop effective strategies based upon the conclusions.

POINTS TO PONDER – SOMETHING TO THINK ABOUT

1. How much information and data do you generally collect on an individual customer or prospect?
2. What mechanisms do you employ to actively review and analyze the information collected on a major account?

TRAINING ACTIVITY – APPLICATION & ACTION PLAN

Select a major account or prospect and develop an account plan based upon the following categories:

- Account goals for the year
- Account objectives by month
- Account call plan
- Planned presentations and demonstrations
- Call plans
- Activities planned between calls
- Post-sale activities
- Schedule of account calls and activities
- Milestones to be achieved

8

Putting Sales Plans into Action

Implementation of a sales plan is all in the execution. When Vince Lombardi coached his fabled Green Bay Packers, he made no bones about his plays. They were simple and straightforward. His team was running straight through the opposition. He knew it, they knew it, but the execution was impeccable. The Packers were difficult to stop. That strategy—execute, execute, execute!—is tough to beat.

IMPLICATIONS – WHAT THIS MEANS TO YOU

Personal effectiveness determines the sales representative's ability to manage their activities and follow their plans. Execution is the key to the success of the sales plan. Salespeople must have the discipline to follow their plans and avoid any major deviation.

This is important because salespeople who successfully execute their plans remain highly motivated. The unmotivated salesperson often fails to effectively execute their plans and adapt to necessary changes. These individuals tend to drift and fail to achieve their goals, objectives and quotas.

STRATEGIES, TIPS & TECHNIQUES TO APPLY

Plans are worthless without a strategy for translating them into action. The following steps should be taken:

Implementation

Sales plans must detail how each goal, objective and strategy will be implemented. Each step must be detailed according to how, why, where and when in order for the salesperson to have a blueprint to follow in achieving their goals and objectives.

Scheduling Activities

Within the framework of their sales and account plans, activities and milestones are planned and scheduled. The first step is to develop a master schedule for the year that details the following activities:

- Scheduled sales calls
- Scheduled sales presentations
- Scheduled product demonstrations
- Scheduled product trials
- Scheduled phone calls
- Scheduled activities between sales calls

Whether placed in a contact management program or in a daily planner, all of the above activities should be detailed for the upcoming 12 months as the sales representative's annual master plan.

Evaluation

Sales plans should have sufficient benchmarks and milestones for salespeople to check their actual performance against projected goals and objectives. These should be established early and frequently enough to allow for corrective action if problems occur or performance lags.

Benchmarks and milestones should be established with the sales manager and be used by both parties to evaluate individual sales performance.

Adaptation

The final step is to adapt the sales plan to actual market conditions and results. As no plan is perfect, modifications will be needed along the way.

Additionally, a plan is never really ever completed, but is a constantly evolving process. The salesperson needs to work the plan and reassess/reestablish goals and objectives on a regular basis.

Time Frame

The most important aspect of sales planning is the initial plan when each step is completely detailed. Once completed, the plan should be revisited quarterly. At that stage, all elements should be reviewed for any alterations, including new customers, new competitors or changes in the sales environment.

A more complete review should be conducted annually, with the entire process repeated every two to three years.

Tactical Planning

Tactical plans should provide the sales representative with an action plan to follow throughout the year. They should detail the monthly objectives to be accomplished— in many cases, broken down into weekly plans. Salespeople should be able to readily follow these plans to guide and direct their activities.

Timelines and sales schedules should be included within the scope of the tactical plan. If salespeople take the time to develop detailed sales plans, it's a simple matter of focusing upon the plan's execution.

The tactical plan should tell salespeople what they are specifically to work on at any given point and time. It should provide a detailed activity schedule, including the milestones to be accomplished weekly and monthly.

Weekly call plans and schedules should be based upon the tactical plans directing the salesperson toward the specific objectives to be accomplished during a given period of time.

Revisions, modifications and adaptations can be made as required to weekly call plans, but salespeople should always be cognizant of the annual strategic plan and their monthly objectives.

Reporting

The weekly call report—the bane of many salespeople—has been making a rapid comeback. Many companies viewed them as a punitive and extraneous form of make-work for many of their people. As companies began to streamline their operations and downsize their staffs, call reports were eliminated as an additional level of unneeded information.

There is a return to accountability—especially since the average cost of sales calls has risen to such a degree that most sales managers are concerned about what is actually going on in the field. However, there is a significant difference between the call report of yesterday and that which is used today.

With the automation of most sales forces, software manufacturers have observed an increasing interest in the generation of useful reports specifically applicable and meaningful to both salespeople and their managers. Without question, most sales representatives and managers are awash in data, but starving for meaningful information they can use and apply.

Today's call report provides the sales manager with a picture of where an individual account is at any given time. It tells the manager where the business is and how close it is to being closed by the salesperson.

A call report can be fashioned to provide information such as a 30-day rolling forecast and activity report as well as a summary of successes, problems, competitive activities and prospecting. Extra reports can be generated on specific details and customers in order to help the salesperson prepare for a sales call with the appropriate support documents.

Regardless of the format used, call reports are becoming sophisticated action plans. The details that salespeople have committed themselves to are logged into their computers, developing the follow-up and to-do lists required to fulfill the promises made to customers. The extra step lies in summarizing these activities and generating them into a call report.

Toilsome call reports are becoming a thing of the past as salespeople learn to maximize their power through the use of existing sales automation software. The call report is a medium of shared information allowing the sales manager to support the selling activities of their people. It is another tool in the sales "bag of tricks" and techniques for success.

POINTS TO PONDER — SOMETHING TO THINK ABOUT

1. How detailed have your annual plans been in the past?
2. How do you use technology to make your planning and follow-up activities easier and more effective?

TRAINING ACTIVITY — APPLICATION & ACTION PLAN

1. Create an annual master plan.
2. Develop a master schedule for the year. The schedule should list the following activities:
    - Scheduled sales calls
    - Scheduled sales presentations
    - Scheduled product demonstrations
    - Scheduled product trials
    - Scheduled phone calls
    - Scheduled activities between sales calls
3. Place all of these activities for the upcoming twelve months in a contact management program or in a daily planner.

About the Author

Timothy F. Bednarz, Ph.D. is CEO of the American Management Development Group, Inc. For over 20 years he has researched, designed and authored hundreds of learning and development programs used by Fortune 1000 companies.

He is also the author of *Great! What Makes Leaders Great. What They Did, How They Did It and What You Can Learn from It* (2011).

Speaking Availability

Timothy F. Bednarz, Ph.D. is available for speaking engagements for your next meeting or association event. He can be contacted at 800-654-4935 or by e-mail at timothy.bednarz@majorium.com.

Bulk Sales

Bulk sales of this book or any other titles available from Majorium Business Press. Inquiries can be directed to sales@majorium.com, or by phone at 800-6654-4935.

Quick Order Form

Fax orders: 715-342-1118. Send this form.

Telephone orders: Call 800-654-4935 toll-free. Have your credit card ready.

Email orders: sales@majorium.com

Postal orders: Majorium Business Press, 2025 Main Street, Stevens Point, WI 54481, USA.

Please send the following books:

____

____

____

____

Please send more FREE information on:

❑Catalog ❑Speaking/Seminars ❑Mailing Lists ❑Consulting

Name: ____________________________________

Address: __________________________________

City: ____________________ State: _____ Zip: __________

Telephone: ________________________________

Email address: ______________________________

Sales tax: Please add 5.5% for products shipped to Wisconsin addresses.

Shipping by air:

United States: $4.00 for first book and $2.00 for each additional product.

International: $9.00 for first book; $5.00 for each additional product (estimate).

Made in United States
Cleveland, OH
06 November 2026

47678360R10030